Table of Contents

Introduction.. 1

Methodology 4

Review of Literature 5

Chapter I: Who is Legally a Terrorist? 13
  Terrorism Legally Defined 13

  The Purpose of Anti-Terror Laws and their Legal Ramifications 17

  Effects of the Law in COIN and Stability Environments 19

  Chapter Summary 22

Chapter II: Strategy or Ideology 23
  Terrorism in History 23

  Terrorism as a Methodology 27

  Assimilation After Terrorism.. 32

  Chapter Summary 36

Chapter III: Case Studies 37
  Mujahedin-e Khalq 37

  Hamas 43

Conclusion 51

Bibliography 55

Introduction

The official categorization of groups and individuals as "terrorist" by the United States (U.S.) Government carries sweeping legal ramifications, some of which indirectly affect military operations. These operations often occur in places where the distinction between a terrorist and a patriot is as vague and perplexing as the political boundaries and district lines within the United States. What or who, therefore, is a terrorist? What are the legal stipulations of this categorization and its impact on military operations? These questions assume significant meaning when conducting operational targeting during irregular warfare. The purpose of this monograph is to assess the relevancy of the "terrorist" categorization in combat and analyze whether or not its legal ramifications have adverse effects on military operations in an asymmetric combat environment.

Asymmetric warfare requires operations be conducted across a broad spectrum almost simultaneously. These operations include sociopolitical targeting for which measures of effectiveness are difficult to define. The proverbial "gray area" is not just another variable in the environment—it is the environment. Additionally, success in asymmetric conflicts requires military operators to place a disproportionate amount of reliance on Inform and Influence Activities (IIA). These activities target the cognitive realm of a demographic to set favorable conditions for civil-military operations. This is one reason why asymmetric warfare is more complex than conventional force on force. Adding to the complexity are the cultural norms in most regions where these types of operations occur. As most international business executives know, acts such as

1

corruption, extortion, and bribery are routine daily affairs in developing nations like Afghanistan and Somalia.[1]

The recent wars in Iraq (2003-present) and Afghanistan (2001-present) highlighted shortfalls in the legacy U.S. military structure. The asymmetric nature of counter-insurgency (COIN) proved taxing on its symmetric, high intensity force-on-force, combat structure. With time, it became apparent that the cold war organization of the military was not ideal for the COIN environment. This warranted a drastic redirection in strategy for prosecution of the Iraq and Afghan wars.

The more information and experience military leaders gained in Afghanistan and Iraq, the more perplexing and unfamiliar the conflict became. Individuals and organizations originally thought to be against American interests suddenly were in line with them.[2] Others believed to support the efforts of the United States were completely opposed to it.[3] The strategic model involving tanks patrolling city and rural streets suddenly did not fit either of the two operational environments.

Strategic changes were necessary in order to improve conditions in both theaters. This included a thorough revamping of the lethal and non-lethal targeting process. The change improved operational targeting, but encountered legal barriers. Certain groups, such as the African National Congress (ANC), whose interests were in line with those of the United States, were listed as terrorists by the Department of State (DoS). This resulted in a series of legal restrictions that handicapped an already anemic targeting process.

---

[1] Charles W. L. Hill, *International Business, Competing in the Global Marketplace*, ed. Brent Gordon, 8th ed., Vol. One (Washington: McGraw-Hill, 2011), 53.
[2] Jeffrey Record, *Beating Goliath: Why Insurgencies Win* (Washington, D.C.: Potomac Books, 2009), 180.
[3] Ibid.

Anti-terrorist restrictions made it difficult—if not illegal—for military leaders to meet with or provide support to certain organizations. As a result, the policy of categorizing groups as terrorists indirectly hindered oversees military operations.

In order to analyze the effect the terrorist categorization has on military operations, this research addresses in the literature review and chapter one the definitional challenges that arise when trying to categorize a terrorist, the official definitions, legal ramifications, and the potential effects on COIN and stability operations. Through an analysis of various historical conflicts and military campaigns, chapter two assesses whether terrorism is a strategy or an ideology—to determine the suitability of U.S Code in the contemporary combat environment. Chapter three assesses the lasting political and operational effects of the label through case studies of the Mujahedin e Khalq (MEK) and Hamas. Finally, the conclusion summarizes the findings from the research and provides recommendations.

Methodology

Interagency policies often results in one branch of a government using resources to overcome the barriers placed by another. While barriers are required, not all are relevant or beneficial. Those that are not contribute to government inefficiency and waste. This research will examine the hypothesis by conducting an analysis of the laws and policies relating to terrorism and juxtaposing them with empirical information on the uses of terrorism. This monograph will also include case studies of organizations on the DoS terror list in order to assess real world implications of U.S. terror laws in combat.

Case studies are constructed using Alexander George and Andrew Bennett's case study methodology. This methodology utilizes the integration of five design tasks to construct case studies. Task one, is specification of the problem and research objective, task two is specification of variables, task three consists of case selection, task four is variances in the variables, and task five is formulation of information.

This monograph uses three forms of references: primary, secondary, and tertiary sources. Primary sources include United States Congress legal documents, DoS policy memorandums, Department of Defense joint publications and policies, and US Army field manuals. Secondary sources include scholarly journals and professional research papers. Tertiary sources consist primarily of news and magazine articles.

The Combined Arms Research Library's database and reference resources are the primary means to gather reference materials and conduct case studies. Government documents are taken from official sources (i.e. legal ramifications for terrorist support are taken from the DoS website or Library of Congress) to ensure validity and accuracy. The independent verification of information uses similar references.

Review of Literature

When Graham Allison coined the phrase "where you stand depends on where you sit,"[4] he may have been attempting to define who a "terrorist" is or what constitute "terrorism". Many books with multiple volumes attempt to define these two terms and the definitions contained within them vary a great deal. Finding an internationally recognized definition proved insurmountable. An Alex Schmid survey identified more than 100 definitions for terrorism.[5] The only consensus amongst the authors is there can be no single, universally agreed upon definition for terrorism or a terrorist.

In addition to academia, the United Nations (U.N.) has taken care not to clearly define terrorism or label anyone a terrorist while the U.S. government provides several definitions for both. Appreciation for the challenges when attempting to define the terms is central to the thesis of this research because military personnel operate within legal parameters established by definitions such as, who is a terrorist and what constitute terrorism. This review will begin at the macro level, which is the global scholar's attempt at a definition, and conclude at the micro level, which in this case is the Department of Defense's Joint Publication definition. This will allow for the comparison of divergent approaches that attempt to address the definitional complexity that surround defining terrorists and terrorism.

---

[4] Graham T. Allison and Philip Zelikow, *Essence of Decision: Explaining the Cuban Missile Crisis*, 2nd ed. (New York: Longman, 1999).
[5] Gus Martin, *Understanding Terrorism: Challenges, Perspectives, and Issues*, 3rd ed. (Los Angeles: Sage, 2010), 41.

Gus Martin, author of *Understanding Terrorism*, stated that defining terrorism is a subjective exercise in semantics.[6] Many scholars share a similar view in regards to attempts at defining the terms. Some place it squarely in the political spectrum and imply that the terrorist label is a pejorative term used by opponents of an actor to influence public or international opinion—thus meaningless when taken out of context.[7] Others believe that terrorism and terrorists are words that insidiously worked their way into the modern (post 1960) lexicon because of inconsistent and myopic international media coverage.[8]

The scholars may not all agree on the root or degree of usefulness for the terms, but they generally share the view that the definition is subjective because terrorists always see themselves as fighters representing an oppressed group.[9] On the other end of the spectrum, critics view terrorists as violent extremist attempting to subvert the rule of law.[10] For this reason, the academic definition of terrorism depends greatly on the area of research and the point of view from which the research is conducted. Middle Eastern scholars like Sayyid Qutb and Abbas Amant may look at the same individual, but define him as a freedom fighter rather than a terrorist. Ultimately, most scholars converge and agree that categorizing an individual or organization without context is hollow.

---

[6] Ibid., 46.

[7] Dan G. Cox, John Falconer, and Brian Stackhouse, *Terrorism, Instability, and Democracy in Asia and Africa* (Hanover, NH: University Press of New England, 2009), 8.

[8] Bruce Hoffman, *Inside Terrorism*, Rev a expa ed. (New York: Columbia University Press, 2006), 30.

[9] Martin, *Understanding Terrorism: Challenges, Perspectives, and Issues*

[10] Ibid., 57.

To the aggressor—often called the terrorist—a revolution is required to change the status quo.[11] During a period of revolution, terror serves to benefit a democracy.[12] Such terror is therefore virtuous, necessary, and void of true evil—in spite of violent acts.[13] Many aggressors avoid the terrorist stigma and use modern adjectives such as guerrilla fighter, freedom fighter, or rebel fighter to distinguish their organization as one with a legitimate cause.[14]

Distinction is important to actors who plan to engage in the international community and therefore great pains are taken to ensure that the terrorist label is not affixed to their cause. A guerrilla fighter or freedom fighter may use indirect tactics but they routinely avoid the overt targeting of civilians or non-combatants.[15] One scholar's hope of removing the ambiguity identified the targeting of civilians as a trait that delineates the lines drawn by terrorist and those drawn by rebel fighters. The targeting of civilians is a common trend among terrorists and therefore a part of the definition should include harm or threat of harm to civilians or non-combatants.[16] This aids in separating the "freedom fighter" from the true terrorist.

Other scholars, even in the context of deliberate targeting of civilians, disagree with any attempts at defining terrorism. The ambiguity in the definition illustrates that terrorism is one type of behavior or action along a continuum of possible behaviors for

---

[11] Thomas S. Kuhn, *The Structure of Scientific Revolutions*, 3rd ed. (Chicago, Ill.: University of Chicago Press, 1996), 112.

[12] Hoffman, *Inside Terrorism*, 4323.

[13] Ibid., 3.

[14] Paul R. Pillar and Inc ebrary, *Terrorism and U.S. Foreign Policy* (Washington, D.C.: Brookings Institution Press, 2001), 17.

[15] Martin, *Understanding Terrorism: Challenges, Perspectives, and Issues*, 49.

[16] Mark Juergensmeyer and Inc NetLibrary, *Terror in the Mind of God*, Vol. 13 (Berkeley: University of California Press, 2000), 6.

individuals who oppose the status quo.[17] Disenfranchised individuals fighting the status quo need to influence public opinion to further their cause.[18] Violence is used and continues to be used because it is an effective form of control; by killing one, a thousand can be controlled.[19] This supports the methodology that the use of violence to influence a population or government is an effective way to produce desired results.[20] Terrorism employs violence or the threat of violence because it is effective and cost beneficial.[21] Therefore, a terrorist, as viewed by some scholars, is a warrior employing unconventional tactics within his means.[22]

The United Nations, with its multi-cultural members, was unsuccessful in developing a definition for who is a terrorist and what constitutes terrorism.[23] The reasons for a lack of consensus are numerous, but in summary, certain members of each committee had concerns that organizations defending their land from an occupying force could be labeled a terrorist. The label would naturally bring with it all the international ramifications, like sanctions and support restrictions. The last counter-terrorism committee to hold a meeting on the subject faced similar concerns by various panel members and closed without deciding on a definition.[24]

---

[17] Pillar and ebrary, *Terrorism and U.S. Foreign Policy*, 17.

[18] Juergensmeyer and NetLibrary, *Terror in the Mind of God*, 5.

[19] Martin, *Understanding Terrorism: Challenges, Perspectives, and Issues*, 57.

[20] Ibid., 57.

[21] Ibid., 17.

[22] Ibid.

[23] United Nation, "AD HOC Committee Negotiating Comprehensive Anti-Terrorism," Department of Public Information, News and Media Division, New York, http://www.un.org/News/Press/docs/2007/L3112.doc.htm (accessed August 20, 2011).

[24] United Nation, "Press Conference by Head of Counter-Terrorism Committee Executive Directorate," Department of Public Information, News and Media Division, New York, http://www.un.org/News/briefings/docs/2010/101201_CTED.doc.htm (accessed August 20, 2011).

The United Nations inability to come to a resolution on the definition of the terms illustrates how difficult it is to define something when viewed differently by different cultures—or people within the same culture but with opposing interest. Palestinians call the Israelis terrorists, Kurdish militants call the Turks terrorists, Tamil militants consider the Indonesian government terrorists and the respective nation-states view their accusers much the same way.

Unlike the United Nations, the United States appeared to have had very little trouble finding multiple definitions for terrorism.[25] Where the former could not produce a single definition, the latter has many. Each differs slightly from the others, but all are broad enough to include anyone living outside the United States that has ever taken part in status quo changing events such as an insurgency, a rebel uprising, civil disobedience, or tribal conflict. The psychologist Charles Ruby, in an article he wrote titled *"The Definition of Terrorism,"* addressed the contextual issue with defining terrorism and implied that hypocrisy is intrinsic to the topic.[26] All virtuously condemn acts of terrorism unless conducted by friends, supporters, or the individuals themselves. In cases where the acts of terror can be related to or understood, the concept is ignored, brushed over, or dampened with phrases such as "revolution" or "defender of freedom."[27] Ruby never arrived at a definition in his article, but suggested that psychological behavior must be factored in to provide a reliable operational definition.[28]

---

[25] Anthony H. Cordesman and Center for Strategic and International Studies, *Terrorism, Asymmetric Warfare, and Weapons of Mass Destruction: Defending the U.S. Homeland* (Westport, Conn.: Praeger, 2002), 40.

[26] Charles L. Ruby, "The Definition of Terrorism," *Analysis of Social Issues and Public Policy* (2002), 9-13.

[27] Ibid.,13.

[28] Ibid.

The U.S. Code states that acts of terror are politically motivated and directed towards noncombatants, but excludes politically motivated acts of terror committed by nation-states.[29] In essence, only non-state actors are considered terrorists according to U.S. law. Nations use violence or the threat of violence to deter acts that are counter to their national interest. Such violence is interpreted as national security and not terrorism.[30] Despite incidences of state sponsored terrorism, there is no legal provision for nations who use proxy terrorists to further their cause—outside of retaliation options. The U.S. Department of State adapts the before mentioned U.S. Code but tailors it to address organizations and individuals residing outside the United States.

Based on U.S. Code and the Department of State's definition, any criminal entity or tribal leader residing outside the United States and using traditional ways to deal with conflicts of interest, meet the criteria to be listed as a terrorist. The Department of Defense's definition is shorter, but equally inclusive. Its definition emphasizes the use of violence to inculcate fear and intimidate societies and governments.[31] The Department of Defense's definition implicates rebel and insurgent organizations as terrorist, much like the U.S. Code. This exemplifies the concerns that Middle Eastern members of the United Nations' counter-terrorism council have.[32] They fear that legitimate uprisings will not get the international recognition they deserve because they were inappropriately categorized by their actions. Most rebel uprisings and insurgencies, by nature, are politically

---

[29] *Definition of Terrorism,* 101, , no. 101, Title 22 (1989, 1988): 2656f(d).

[30] Office of the Coordinator for Counterterrorism, "U.S. State Department Foreign Terrorist Organization List," U.S. Department of State, http://www.state.gov/s/ct/rls/other/des/123085.htm (accessed September, 2011).

[31] Department of Defense, *Joint Publication 3-26, Counterterrorism* (Washington, DC: Department of Defense, 2009), 125. GL-10.

[32] United Nation, *Press Conference by Head of Counter-Terrorism Committee Executive Directorate,* 1.

motivated and violate the established laws of their government. Therefore, most of these groups would also meet the Department of Defense's criteria for terrorist classification.

The asymmetric nature of the modern battlefield means military organizations will maneuver in a multi-cultural and multi-tribal quagmire inundated with individuals who do not fit into U.S. legal and doctrinal categories. The landscape of the environment exposes the military to individuals belonging to organizations that often meet the terrorist criteria by the Department of State, Department of Defense, or both. This renders support to, or coordination with, these organizations illegal. This produces additional challenges for military planners and places military leaders in a precarious situation when operating on the ground. For planners, the best option that supports strategic objectives may be diluted, reducing its intended effect, while leaders are restricted from coordinating with individuals who influence their area of operation.

Although military leaders must always ensure they obey the laws of warfare, those laws were intended to limit events in war such as lethal employment options, poor treatment of prisoners, and collateral damage.[33] In essence, the defined laws of warfare were constructed around protecting defenseless individuals in a force on force model and have limited provisions for non-lethal engagement. Terrorism, as defined by national level authority, serves to aid in the protection of the United States from the aggression of non-state actors. The definition thus becomes desultory in many areas outside U.S borders where the military is presently operating. The current (2011) United States involvement in Afghanistan is an example where ground operators conduct a balancing

---

[33] Terry D. Gill and Dieter Fleck, *Handbook of the International Law of Military Operations* (Oxford ; New York: Oxford University Press, 2010), 657.

act between what is strategically beneficial and what is legal. Attempts to define individuals and groups as terrorist who are opposed to U.S. national interests have proved challenging. In places like Afghanistan, tradition and tribal ties influence how the population employs violence. Violent acts that would meet the terror criteria by the U.S. definition are legitimate retaliation methods in the Afghan culture.[34]

Further, the myriad of definitions at the national and international levels have the potential to lead to inconsistent application during military operations, which can adversely affect the desired end state. Combatants that engage the military have little concern for Western definitions.[35] The threat of a Western label does not serve as an incentive for them to change their chosen ways of fighting, especially when it appears to produce the desired result.[36] When placed in the proper context of time, circumstances, resources, and opponent capability, acts of terror appear more logical than maniacal. The contextual gap in the U.S. definitions of who a terrorist is and what constitutes terrorism raises a question of the applicability of the definition during combat operations in asymmetric environments.

---

[34] Record, *Beating Goliath: Why Insurgencies Win*, 180.
[35] Martin, *Understanding Terrorism: Challenges, Perspectives, and Issues*
[36] Hoffman, *Inside Terrorism*, 432.

Chapter I: Who is Legally a Terrorist?

As discussed in the review of literature, defining terrorism is a subjective exercise, but for legal purposes, a definition is required. This chapter will review the legal definitions relating to terrorism, the implications that accompany these definitions, and the effects—if any—on military operators in a non-linear combat environment.

Terrorism Legally Defined

Scholars and bureaucrats notwithstanding, the average person would deduce that a terrorist is someone who commits or engages in acts of terror. While logical, it leads to the problem of identifying what constitutes acts of terror. Terror is not easily defined and what one group calls terrorism another calls warfare. The often used phrase "one man's terrorist is another's freedom fighter" exemplifies this.[37] With no unanimous agreement—not even within the U.S. government—on what acts constitute terrorism, the State Department definition is used as the primary source of reference for this monograph. This definition is chosen because it mirrors U.S. Code and it has overarching legal jurisdiction that supersedes definition from other agencies.[38]

The U.S. State Department's definition includes all the legally binding aspects outlined by U.S. Codes.[39] It, therefore, serves as a comprehensive source for designation, legal criteria, and legal ramifications as it relates to terrorism and the laws surrounding it. The Department of State's list of terrorist organizations is known as the Foreign Terrorist

---

[37] Matthew Carr, *The Infernal Machine: A History of Terrorism* (New York: New Press, 2006), 410.

[38] Office of the Coordinator for Counterterrorism, *U.S. State Department Foreign Terrorist Organization List*, 2.

[39] 22 U.S.C265 legal ramifications The actual laws in its entirety is extremely long and detailed and therefore not placed in this monograph. The entire law can be viewed on the library of Congress website or The Department of State terrorism site; both are provided as references in this monograph.

Organization List (FTOL) or the Terrorist Exclusion List (TEL).[40] In order to be placed

on the list, an individual or organization must meet the following:

1. A foreign organization.

2. Must engage in terrorist activity as defined in section 140(d)(2) of the Foreign Relations Authorization Act, Fiscal Years 1988 and 1989, or retain the capability and intent to engage in terrorist activity or terrorism. (see next paragraph).

3. Must threaten the security of U.S. nationals or the national security (national defense, foreign relations, or the economic interests) of the United States.

Terrorist activities as defined by section 140(d)(2) of the Foreign Relations. Authorization Act, Fiscal Years 1988 and 1989, [41] are as follows:

Any activity which is unlawful under the laws of the place where it is committed (or which, if committed in the United States, would be unlawful under the laws of the United States or any State) and which involves any of the following:

a. The highjacking or sabotage of any conveyance (including an aircraft, vessel, or vehicle).

b. The seizing or detaining, and threatening to kill, injure, or continue to detain, another individual in order to compel a third person (including a governmental organization) to do or abstain from doing any act as an explicit or implicit condition for the release of the individual seized or detained.

c. A violent attack upon an internationally protected person (as defined in section 1116(b)(4) of title 18, United States Code) or upon the liberty of such a person.

d. An assassination.

e. The use of any--biological agent, chemical agent, or nuclear weapon or device, or explosive, firearm, or other weapon or dangerous device (other than for mere personal monetary gain), with intent to endanger, directly or

---

[40] 104th Congress, "Title 18, Crimes and Criminal Procedures, Sec. 2339A. Providing Material Support to Terrorists," Office of the Law Revision Counsel, U.S. House of Representatives, http://uscode.house.gov/uscode-cgi/fastweb.exe?getdoc+uscview+t17t20+1114+36++%28%29%20%20AND%20%28USC%20w%2F10%20%2818%20U.S.C.%20§%202339A%29%29%3ACITE%20%20%20%20%20%20%20%20 (accessed July, 2011).
[41] Ibid.

indirectly, the safety of one or more individuals or to cause substantial damage to property.

    f.   A threat, attempt, or conspiracy to engage in terrorist activity.

The above criteria and definitions are extensive and detailed but lack context. [42] Context is possibly the most important aspect when defining something as subjective as terrorism. It has the potential to include a large number of organizations and individuals that may not deserve the label. Definitions based on behavior and not the context of that behavior can result in anyone labeled a terrorist. For example, a person or group only has to meet one criterion to be on the FTOL. This makes it applicable to a wide range of individuals or groups that military forces engage within COIN environments.

For example, the above criteria that states a person must have used, or retain the use of any "…explosive, firearm, or other weapon or dangerous device…" to be listed on the FTOL, would alienate enough inhabitants to make it almost impossible to conduct COIN in places like Iraq and Afghanistan. In these countries, firearms or dangerous devices are as common as minivans in America, rendering most local leaders terrorist under this broad definition. While it may be uncommon for the average American to have an assault rifle and some explosives stored inconspicuously next to the kitchen table, that is the reality on the ground for the modern military operator in the COIN environment. In Iraq, for example, most houses have at least one type of firearm[43] because tribal skirmishes are frequent and it is common for men of military age to protect their family—and if required, defend their tribe.

---

[42] Ibid.
[43] Terrorism Files, "The History of Terrorism," Nabou, www.terrorismfiles.org/encyclopedia/history (accessed July, 2011).

15

Tribal clashes have a political motive and more often than not harm bystanders, making such clashes acts of terror as well. The perception of tolerable loss of life and legitimate targets varies significantly outside most developed nations. Assessing acceptable methods to use for a struggle through a modern western lens causes inductive categorizations that have little meaning in developing countries, or nations in post conflict. To illustrate this point, the example of how native Africans in apartheid South Africa went from being terrorists to symbols of freedom and social evolution is used.

The situation in Apartheid South Africa serves as an example of how lack of context can play a role in the false categorization of a group challenging the status quo. Native South Africans, as members of the African National Congress (ANC), fought for civil liberties against the national regime, and in doing so, met the criteria and were listed as terrorists by the State Department until 2008.[44] Nelson Mandela, the renowned member of the ANC and Nobel Prize laureate, became president of South Africa in 1994 and is celebrated internationally as one of the most prolific and revolutionary leaders of the 20th century. Mandela received all these awards and accolades—many of which originated from the United States—while being listed as a terrorist by the DoS. He was flagged to prevent access to the United States and barred from receiving support from anyone under U.S. jurisdiction.[45]

In summary, it is possible that the actions of a terrorist and a defender of freedom merge in certain instances. Taken out of context and judged against an arbitrary definition, many people who are positive international role models or key players during

---

[44] Mimi Hall, "U.S. has Mandela on Terrorist List," USA Today, http://www.usatoday.com/news/world/2008-04-30-watchlist_N.htm (accessed July, 2011).
[45] Ibid.

stability or COIN operations would fall into the terrorist category. The lack of context in defining the term is a main reason why a clear distinction between the terrorist and defender of freedom may never know unanimity.

The Purpose of Anti-Terror Laws and their Legal Ramifications

For the military, distinguishing between a terrorist and a freedom fighter is very important. The distinction ensures that military leaders do not inadvertently violate federal law by supporting or funding terrorist activities. The definitions of terrorism may appear ambiguous, but the laws governing interaction with terrorists are explicit. The prosecutorial penalties are severe and military procedures are designed to ensure strict adherence to U.S. Codes.[46] This section will review the intended purpose—the counter argument—and background of the laws that cover terrorism and the legal ramifications inherent to them.

The anti-terror laws served and continue to serve a purpose. The intention of laws is to protect the interests of the nation from aggressive non-state actors.[47] The logic behind the detailed definition of who is a terrorist and what constitutes terrorism is to prevent affiliates of terrorist organizations from attacking, entering, or receiving support from the United States.[48] The laws also serve to protect U.S. personnel globally. The FTOL is the official document that informs allies and those under U.S. jurisdiction which organizations to avoid.[49]

---

[46] Department of Defense, *Joint Publication 3-26, Counterterrorism*, 125.
[47] 101st United States Congress, *Definition of Terrorism*, 2656f(d)-265f(d)
[48] Ibid.
[49] Daniel Benjamin and Steven Simon, *The Age of Sacred Terror*, 1st ed. (New York: Random, 2002), 220-255.

Like all nations, the United States encounters dissident organizations with diverging interest. The presence of these organizations—despite their proliferation since the 1950s—became palpable to most Americans in the 1980s due to a series of terror attacks.[50] Events such as the 1983 Marine Barracks bombing in Beirut, the 1985 Achille Lauro hijacking in Egypt, and the 1988 Lockerbie bombing of a PanAm flight over Scotland contributed to current anti-terror legislations.[51] Within the legislation is authorization for the Secretary of State to designate and maintain a list of individuals and organizations suspected of affiliation with terror.[52]

The ramifications for association with designated organizations are lucid and extensive; covering every imaginable form of relationship one group may have with another. For example, it is unlawful for any person(s) subject to the jurisdiction of the United States to provide support to listed terrorist organizations or individuals.[53] The term support is broad and open to interpretation; therefore, the U.S. Code defines it in more detail to reduce the chances of private interests leading to convenient interpretation. 18 U.S.C. § 2339A(b)(1) states that support includes any property, service, lodging, training, expert advice, weapons, and just about every other conceivable forms of "material support" imaginable.[54] The FTOL facilitates the legal boundaries that reduce the chances of supporting enemy organizations.

---

[50] Files, *The History of Terrorism*, 1.
[51] Ibid.
[52] Ibid.
[53] 104th Congress, *Title 18, Crimes and Criminal Procedures, Sec. 2339A. Providing Material Support to Terrorists*, 2.
[54] Ibid.

The United States, like any other nation, does not want its tax dollars funding its enemies or its citizens inadvertently providing assistance or information. The intent of the FTOL is to aid in reducing the likelihood of an unwitting citizen abetting terrorist groups in their cause.[55] It also serves as a screening criterion to reduce exposure of official representatives of the United States to individuals linked to extreme organizations.

In closing, the Foreign Relations Authorization Act and other laws that govern interaction with terrorist organizations serve an important role in protecting U.S. allies and citizens from attack. The intent of the laws is to make it difficult for individuals associated with terrorism to receive support in the global community and reduce their ability to execute acts of terror on a large scale.

Effects of the Law in COIN and Stability Environments

As previously discussed, definitions without context are hollow and thus open to interpretation. What resembles acts of terrorism through a western lens may be a way of life in other parts of the world. Sectarian tension is rampant in developing countries and like rivaling street gangs in the west, it is difficult to tell when, where, or why it started. Groups in need of money or weapons to defend themselves against other aggressive groups will not hesitate to align themselves—wittingly or unwittingly—with organizations known for using terrorism.[56] The purpose of this section is to evaluate the impact the definitions of terrorism and its legal constraints have on military operators in COIN and Stability environments.

---

[55] Ibid.

[56] Bard E. O'Neill, *Insurgency and Terrorism: From Revolution to Apocalypse*, 2nd ed. (Washington, D.C.: Potomac Books, 2005), 231.

Insurgency by its nature involves a weaker group fighting against a stronger.[57] The immediate threat of a nearby rival eclipses future ramifications of association with groups barred by the United States.[58] As a result, a number of local leaders during the course of an insurgency make alliances that serve their immediate interest. At the same time, military operators navigate the gray area between rivaling groups to find common ground in an attempt to start the stabilization process. This requires comprehensive engagement with all key players in the region. Listing key players or organizations, as terrorists renders most engagements illegal—unless using lethal means of engagement.

The tenuous nature of an asymmetric environment does not lend itself to rigid well-defined categories. Key players seldom fit conveniently into categories of terrorist or freedom fighter. Military planners are forced to develop a one-place/one time adaptive method in order to deal with the unique complexities of the COIN and stability areas of operation.

Applying legal definitions in complex environments is potentially counterproductive and costly. Counterproductive because, it removes key players from viable options conducive to the end state and costly because, removing viable options results in protracted efforts that consume blood and treasure for all involved. Navigating the cultural and political spectrums of a COIN environment requires interacting with individuals that do not meet the western benchmark for scruples.[59] This creates an ethical

---

[57] Ibid.71-91.
[58] Ibid.
[59] Jack Marr et al., "Human Terrain Mapping: A Critical Step to Winning the COIN Fight," *Military Review* 1 (June 28, 2011, 2008), 4.

tension for U.S. military members because, operational necessity may require negotiating with or supporting individuals legally precluded from either.

It is seldom easy to ascertain someone's prior affiliations in places where stability operations or COIN are conducted.[60] These operations are inherently multifarious and often occur where little to no legal infrastructure or centralized archives exist. This renders forensic profiling untenable—at least initially—for military operators attempting to gather information on individuals. Terrorist groups seldom maintain publically accessible activity logs or agendas, therefore, time, relationship building, and use of human intelligence (HUMIT) is the only way to learn who the key players are, the interests they have, and their current and past affiliations. Additionally, information gathering sometimes lead to favorable options for ground forces. Leaders must react quickly within small windows of opportunity when conditions on the ground are conducive to the overall success of the mission. There is little time to file exceptions to policies or conduct a legal review outside the rules of engagement (ROE) to verify that all individuals involved meet the legal criteria for support.

The 2006 Sunni Awakening in Iraq is an example of conditions developing that appear conducive to U.S. strategic interests. Military leaders were faced with two distinct choices: Exploit the rift between Al Qaeda in Iraq (AQI) and Sunnis by supporting Sunnis with alleged links to insurgent and terrorist activities, in order to defeat AQI, or continue along the previous line of effort that was producing marginal results against AQI. Coalition forces decided to provide support to the Sunnis and AQI was defeated, illustrating that when taken into context, organizations can be beneficial.

---

[60] Ibid.

In conclusion, military leaders make decisions based on information currently available, but a rigid definition based system limits options a leader can use to exploit that information. Limited options, in turn, contribute to capricious decisions, which lead to protracted conflicts that increase cost. This results in objectives being "modified" to accelerate a resolution due to a lack of will to continue.

Chapter Summary

Context is critical when defining subjective terms and the lack of context in the U.S Code definition for terrorism allows for a wide categorization of individuals and organizations. These individuals and organizations are an important part of the operational environment when conducting COIN and stability operations. The logic for the laws is sound and it serves to protect U.S. citizens and interests all over the world. The laws and its detail definitions also make it more difficult for terror organizations to gain support from the United States and its allies. The usefulness and intent, however, comes into question when U.S. Code is applied in a combat environment. Its ability to restrict options to the point of retarding progress during COIN and stability operations is counter-productive and, therefore, oppose to the very interests it was intended to serve.

Chapter II: Strategy or Ideology

The purpose of this chapter is to assess whether terrorism is culturally specific or a strategy employed by various cultures. Culturally specific would mean that terrorism is inseparable from the ideology that employs it, but if it is a strategy, then the act—for targeting purposes—can be separated from the ideology that uses it. This chapter will review periods in history when western actors reverted to acts of terror in order to serve their interests, the method behind the terror, and how actors associated with terror assimilate back into the international community—while attempting to distance themselves from their previous malefactions.

<u>Terrorism in History</u>

Terrorism has been in practice for as long as there has been a powerful entity attacking or subjugating a weaker. Philosopher Edmund Burke coined the modern interpretation of the word terrorism. He used the phrase *regime de la terreur* (reign of terror) in his description of atrocities carried out by the Jacobin dictatorship (June 1793 to July 1794) during the French Revolution.[61] The historical references to strategic and tactical uses of terrorism are abundant. Previously named, pillaging, tyrannicide, regicide, and more recently anarchy,[62] acts of terror trace back to the period of antiquity. Historians such as Xenophon (431-350 B.C.) wrote of the psychological terror a small group can have on a population and subsequently shift the balance of power.[63]

---

[61] Martin, *Understanding Terrorism: Challenges, Perspectives, and Issues*, 23.
[62] Ibid., 24.
[63] Files, *The History of Terrorism*, 1.

In the interest of brevity, the historical examples of terrorism will be limited to the period between 1600s-1900s. This period will allow for an assessment of whether or not capabilities, geographical limitations, and opponent strength influence the employment of terrorism, or is it committed for the act itself.[64] The focus is on cultures generally not associated with terrorism to further determine if historical evidence supports the theory that acts of terror are acultural (transcend culture).

The American War of Independence (1775-1783) produced some of the most iconic figures in American history. Before the revolutionary war became a force on force conflict with muskets and howitzers between colonials and British forces, it was, by modern definition, an insurgency.[65] Insurgents, in this case the colonials, used tactics to garner support for their cause that would be illegal by every measure of the current U.S. Code.[66] Citizens who did not support the rebels—a name assigned to colonials by British aristocracy—were often threatened, beaten, tarred, or hung by the rebel forces.[67] Those unfortunate enough to be examples remained on public display to sway the undecided, known as fence sitters.[68] Those openly neutral had their houses burned and crops destroyed or stolen. The purpose was to inflict psychological trauma, illustrate England's inability to secure them, and influence the fence sitters to support the insurgency.[69]

---

[64] Stuart Gottlieb, *Debating Terrorism and Counterterrorism: Conflicting Perspectives on Causes, Contexts, and Responses* (Washington, DC: CQ Press, 2010), 395.

[65] Michael D. Pearlman, "The American Revolutionary War: A Complex "Little Conflict" on the Edge of "the Civilized World"," *US Army Command and General Staff College* 3, no. 3 (November 2010, 2010), 61.

[66] Record, *Beating Goliath: Why Insurgencies Win*, 25-34.

[67] Michael D. Pearlman, "The American Revolutionary War: A Complex "Little Conflict" on the Edge of "the Civilized World"," *US Army Command and General Staff College* 3, no. 3 (November 2010, 2010).

[68] Ibid.

[69] Ibid.

Native Americans, like the weaker colonials fighting the stronger British, adapted measures that meet the legal definition of terrorism. A few Native American tribes, fighting against a perceived existential threat, reverted to unconventional strikes that targeted towns and villages populated with non-combatants.[70] Victims of similar attacks themselves, they resorted to drastic measures as European settlers encroached on their land and negotiations failed.

The Powhatans (also known as Pamunkey) Indians killed 347 English men, women, and children throughout the Virginia colony in 1622.[71] In 1813, Red Stick's Indians killed 400 civilians—scalping 250—at Fort Mims, Alabama. The raids were done to deter settlers from expanding and encourage others to stay out of Indian territory. Though aggressive Native American tribes did the same to other Native Americans, the intent behind their actions did not change; strike fear and terror in the hearts and minds of the opponents and send a clear message to the targeted audience.

Copious examples of terrorism by European settlers saturate historical archives. Colonial expansion created a real estate conflict between natives and colonists and it soon became apparent to the colonists that their further expansion is restricted by the land treaties they drafted. In order to violate the treaty and encourage a westward migration of Native Americans, the colonists sought to make it inhospitable for natives near colonial settlements. The methods adopted meet all definitions for terrorism today.

---

[70] William M. Osborn, *The Wild Frontier*, 1st ed., Vol. 1 (New York: Random House, 2000), 309.
[71] Ibid.

The 1637 Mystic and 1643 Pavonia massacres resulted in the deaths of almost 1,000 sleeping or surrendered women and children.[72] Their deaths were executed in a particularly horrific way—burned alive—to send a clear message and create an environment of terror among Native Americans in the area.[73] An environment of terror and fear among the Native American community encouraged them to leave their lands and move further west, meeting the intent of the settlers.

The use of terrorism was not limited to the continental United States, or to westerners. In 1879, a group of Russian students opposed to a czarist form of government embarked on a reign of terror that lasted for more than two years.[74] The group, known as Narodnaya Volya (The People's Will), conducted widespread shootings, knifings, bombings and a number of other violent acts against everyone from a peasant to the Czar himself. The group wanted to start a popular uprising (insurgency) that would result in a communist form of government, which they believed would serve the people better than an Imperial State. They believed the systematic removal of incumbent officials combined with civil disturbance was the fastest way to bring about change. The group continued on their reign of terror until they assassinated Alexander II in 1881.[75]

More recently, the Japanese Red Army (JRA), a 1970s group in support of Palestinian nationalism, selected acts of terror to further their cause. The group originated from a 1960s student protest movement against the Japanese government, the U.S.

---

[72] Ibid.
[73] Ibid.
[74] Martin, *Understanding Terrorism: Challenges, Perspectives, and Issues.*
[75] Ibid., 26.

military presence in Japan, and the Vietnam War.[76] Seeing no impact from the protest or

political persuasion, the group aligned itself with the international communist movement

and hijacked a Japan Airlines plane, forcing the pilots to fly to North Korea.[77] The

success of the hijacking led to JRA members attacking Ben-Gurion Airport near Tel

Aviv, killing passengers in the terminal and attempting to blow up a plane. They

successfully killed 23 people and injured 80.[78]

In summary, authors such as Patrick Porter[79] and John A. Lynn[80] have argued that

interests and an opponent's strength determine tactics as much as culture and capability.

The employment of terror tactics is, therefore, acultural. Colonists used burning and

hangings, the Indians preferred scalping, and the Asians used bullets and bombs. The

tools and methods of execution vary as much as the names but they all serve the same

purpose: to influence a demographic through fear. Stuart Gottlieb stated that in the

subjective world of terrorism, justifying killing depends on who is doing the justifying.[81]

For Easterners, Westerners, and Natives, justification hinges on interests.

Terrorism as a Methodology

Bruce Hoffman, a leading author on terrorism, emphasized that terrorist attacks—

contrary to popular belief and media depiction—are carefully planned and designed to

---

[76] Harvey W. Kushner, "Japanese Red Army," Encyclopedia of Terrorism, www.google.books/books (accessed November 24, 2011).
[77] Ibid.
[78] Ibid.
[79] Patrick Porter, *Military Orientalism: Eastern War through Western Eyes* (New York: Columbia University Press, 2009), 263.
[80] John A. Lynn, *Battle: A History of Combat and Culture*, Rev a updat ed. (Cambridge, MA: Westview Press, 2004), 431.
[81] Gottlieb, *Debating Terrorism and Counterterrorism: Conflicting Perspectives on Causes, Contexts, and Responses*, 395.

communicate a message. The plan fits the aim of the group, within its capabilities, and takes into account the "targeted audience."[82] Hoffman further noted that there is one commonality among terrorist "they do not commit actions randomly or senselessly."[83] Not even the popular perception that suicide bombers are mindless social misfits is accurate. Most are average or above average for their community both in social status and intelligence.[84] As the knowledge of why terror is used as a course of action becomes widely known, a separation can be made between strategic goals and the ideology that fuels the acts of terrorism.

Many of these insurgent organizations lack the resources and capabilities of most western nations, and thus resort to acts of terrorism to serve their interest. This is not an attempt to justify terrorism as a course of action, but simply an attempt at objective operation analysis. The options available to insurgents are limited by design, or they would conduct high intensity conflicts, not an insurgency. Larbi Ben M'Hidi, a captured insurgent from the Algeria National Liberation Front in 1957, expressed the lack of options succinctly: "It would be better if we too had planes. Give me the bombers, and you can have the [exploding] baskets."[85] Lacking access to equipments such as howitzers, tanks, and anti-aircraft weapons insurgents resort to terror to cause a shift in the status quo.

---

[82] Hoffman, *Inside Terrorism*, 229.
[83] Ibid., 173.
[84] Robert Anthony Pape, *Dying to Win: The Strategic Logic of Suicide Terrorism*, 1st ed. (New York: Random House, 2005), 335.
[85] Gottlieb, *Debating Terrorism and Counterterrorism: Conflicting Perspectives on Causes, Context, and Responses*, 67.

Palpable shifts—perceived or real—in the status quo cause a reaction by everyone affected in the system. Depending on the extent, the population disenfranchised by the shift may resort to extreme measures. Steven Metz's publication by the *Strategic Studies Institute* stated that insurgencies come to fruition when the gap between expectations and opportunity become unacceptable.[86] Individuals or groups then choose from an array of options they believe will serve their interests. The trend is the more connected and well-funded groups will employ a hybrid tactic in which violence and bureaucracy combines for a synergetic effect. Less monetarily endowed groups may opt for just violence or bureaucracy. Those whom the status quo favors will view the insurgent group as terrorists while others not so fortunate may view them as revolutionaries.

For powerful nations, insurgents are akin to a mosquito in a dark room. The buzzing is constant and bites felt immediately, but there is reluctance to turn on the lights and wake everyone. Instead, enervated countermeasures are selected to keep the insistent bug at bay. In other words, the view of insurgent warfare is of an annoying inconvenience requiring limited effort and commitment of resources.[87] Insurgents view things a little differently. To them, it is a matter of great importance and they want all the lights on to address their concerns. The perpetrators of terror also believe these are warranted acts

---

[86] Steven Metz and Army War College . Strategic Studies Institute, *Rethinking Insurgency* (Washington, D.C.: Congressional Research Service, Library of Congress, 2007), 69.
[87] Loren B. Thompson, *Low-Intensity Conflict: The Pattern of Warfare in the Modern World* (Lexington, Mass.: Lexington Books, 1989), 207.

because they perceive the threat as existential.[88] With that in mind, any and every option is on the table and can be justifiably used.[89]

Non-state actors who feel threatened by a state to the point of violent insurgency will do everything to avoid a direct confrontation with the state. Direct confrontations favor the national forces, so drawing attention to the cause is done in other ways. Acts of terror are phenomenal attention-getters and that more than any other reason is why it is used, despite its brutality and inherent risks to the perpetrator.[90] Most—if not all—individuals currently using terrorism would rather choose another more effective and less risky way of drawing attention to a cause and gaining support. Research indicates that groups that use terror with no political or social motives fail to gain the long-term support required to further their cause. As a result, they are unable to launch a sustained campaign of terror against their opponent. Care is thus taken to ensure the targeted audience receives the intended message, thereby giving purpose to the act.

The resurgence of the use of religion to galvanize individuals to a cause meets the social—and in some cases political—requirement to muster support. If an act of terror can be viewed as a struggle for religious rights and not just anarchy, others of that same religion are more likely to support the effort.

Attempts at distinguishing Western acts of aggression from those of others is one of the reasons many scholars, like Qutb and Ruby, argue that a double standard exists. In essence, the West appears hypocritical when it uses a method, benefit from it, define it in

---

[88] Russell D. Howard, Reid L. Sawyer, and Barry R. McCaffrey, *Terrorism and Counterterrorism: Understanding the New Security Environment : Readings & Interpretations* (Guilford, CT: McGraw-Hill, 2002), 389.
[89] Thompson, *Low-Intensity Conflict: The Pattern of Warfare in the Modern World*, 207.
[90] Hoffman, *Inside Terrorism*, 234.

such a way that it excludes them (States cannot be considered terrorist according to U.S. Code), and then condemn its use by others. Advocates of terrorism argue terror acts are a way to further a cause and see no difference between it and previous acts committed by the West. Like bombing and the use of artillery, terrorism is a tactic used to achieve a desired goal, and not an ideological reason for existence.

Individuals identified as terrorist do not see themselves that way. Evidence shows that most perpetrators who commit acts of terror see their actions as heroic blows against an imposing organization.[91] They know and understand how the West views them and therefore use the word "terrorist" to demonstrate their resolve. Labeling them with a pejorative term will do little to shake their will or deter them from the use of their preferred course of action. Separating individuals and organizations from their chosen way to wage conflict allows for non-lethal targeting to address the cognitive variables— like ideology—and lethal to defeat the executors. This produces a synergetic affect that is dependent on both, lethal and non-lethal, being executed concurrently. Restricting non-lethal options due to legal constraints may have an effect on the timeliness of achieving the end-state, possibly making it unattainable.

In summary, terrorism is a tactic or methodology used by individuals and organizations to draw attention to a particular source of friction. Acts of terror historically fail to unilaterally provide decisive victory for its perpetrator. They are simply a way— some argue the fastest—to get an opponent to the negotiating table or to garner support for a cause. Separating the strategic employment of terrorism from the perpetrator's

---

[91] Strobe Talbott and Nayan Chanda, *The Age of Terror: America and the World After September 11*, 1st ed. (New York: Basic Books : Yale Center for the Study of Globalization, 2001), 25.

ideology allows for more accurate targeting (lethal and non-lethal) and facilitates a timely achievement of the desired end-state.

<u>Assimilation After Terrorism</u>

The purpose of this section is to explore how certain actors shed the terrorist moniker and what role, if any, the military plays. This section also serves as a prelude to the next chapter's case study of two organizations trying to separate their previous transgressions from their current and future ambitions.

Native Americans and European settlers, despite deep-seated differences, reconciled and negotiated a resolution, albeit a contentious one. History shows that groups take drastic measures when situations appear drastic, but assimilating into the international community after being associated with acts of terror is nonetheless possible.

The duration for assimilation carries the charge of hypocrisy by scholars as well because the process takes much longer for Eastern acts of terror than those of the West. A terror act committed by the West is called war crimes, and often forgiven shortly after the investigation closes. The same act committed by an eastern group, like Hamas, is labeled terrorism and branded for decades with little chance for assimilation into the international community.

Critics of terrorism argue that there exists a distinct difference between terrorism and war crimes. Martin and Hoffman support this argument by pointing out that in instances where war crimes are committed, there is an attempt—tepid or otherwise—by the military to prosecute individuals or organizations involved. An alternate view on terrorism, like those of Qutb and Amant,[92] states that to prosecute or not is a moot point because the damage from the act has been done. The perpetrator of the action and the organization have already benefited or been disadvantaged by the cognitive fallout.

How long the fallout lasts depends on a number of variables. The Native Americans, colonists, and Russian students all committed their acts of terror in a long gone era. No one living today has any first hand cognitive trauma from their reign of terror. With time, memory of the violent acts fade and a new perception of all involved develop.

Time, therefore, facilitates an organization's ability to change its image, but in addition to time, the palpable impact created by images of the acts of terror is also a factor in assimilation. Scholars argue that the modern twenty-four-hour news cycle makes it difficult for organizations to move on from decisions they made during times of desperation.[93] Organizations that committed terror acts prior to the advent of networked media and near-real-time news were not concerned with residual fallout for failure to meet a predetermined moral benchmark.[94]

Technology provides a medium for acts of terror committed today, on another continent, to be streamed to anyone with a media device. Scholars such as Hoffman supports the argument that the twenty-four-hour news cycle has contributed to myopic state level policies towards groups who use primitive methods to achieve their goals. This they surmise, is in part due to the media's ability to provide graphic images of events

---

[92] Ibid., 37.
[93] Hoffman, *Inside Terrorism*, 432.
[94] Ibid.

from across the world making cruelty and suffering of victims of terror more palpable to westerners far removed from the context surrounding the act itself.

A nation or group trying to distance itself from previous negative behavior may find the media barrage overwhelming. If that organization lacks the political leverage to overcome the media's influence, it may never be widely accepted into the international community. Another determination of whether or not the moniker sticks depends greatly on the outcome of the conflict.[95] If the rebel-freedom fighting-terrorist group ends up being the ruling body of a nation, then the duration to legitimacy may be shortened. This, however, was not the case with the Palestinian organization Hamas.

For groups such as Hamas, past acts of terror continue to plague plans for future statehood. The Hamas situation remains a point of consternation in the Middle East because of their direct opposition to Israel and subsequently the United States. Technology is used globally to drum up support for or against the legitimacy of Hamas by flooding media devices with information about past acts of bravery (for) or terror (against) that they committed.

The Mujahedin-e Khalq (MEK) is another group, attempting to distance itself from past acts of terror. For the MEK, their acts of terror predate modern media, so few outside of the government know the group. Aware of this, the MEK employs methods such as lobbying and press releases with revised narratives to increase support for their path to assimilation and ultimately, legitimacy. Gaining legitimacy in the international community is important for organizations wanting to gain power and keep it. In addition to the financial benefits such as legalized trade deals and access to markets, legitimacy

---

[95] Martin, *Understanding Terrorism: Challenges, Perspectives, and Issues*, 57.

provides a degree of security. For groups like the MEK and Hamas, legitimacy would serve as a deterrent for their enemies because of the coalition associated with it. For example, Hamas on the FTOL provides Israel with more engagement options to attack Palestine than if Hamas was viewed as a legitimate government.

In instances where the military—or what was perceived as the legitimate military arm of the group—terrorize a population, public prosecution for violator(s) is another way groups or nations attempt expiation. The Abu Ghraib[96] prison controversy, while not defined by U.S. Code as an act of terror, serves as an example of a nation attempting to repair its image by not only officially condemning the act, but also swiftly prosecuting offenders. Leaders then ensure information about corrective action is disseminated to the affected populous to encourage dialogue between members of the military and the community. Thus, in addition to time and media depiction, discourse is also a factor when attempting to assimilate.

In closing, a comprehensive approach appears best when dealing with terror activists attempting to assimilate into the international community. Some organizations are more apt at distancing themselves from previous acts of terror and gain acceptance—and with it legitimacy—sooner than others. Time, public perception through media depiction, and discourse, all play a role in an organization's ability to start the process of removing the stain of previous malefactions.

---

[96] An Army Specialist turned over hundreds of pictures of detainee mistreatment by coalition members in Iraq. The viral images became a moral scar on Coalition forces and the United States.

<u>Chapter Summary</u>

Terrorism is a strategy used, by weaker opponents, from various cultures, to facilitate the meeting of their objectives. Military operators have the ability to tailor the targeting process to address the strategic side of terrorism, as well as, the ideology that employs it. History shows that in drastic times, cultures adapt drastic measures. In spite of these measures, the military must work with all involved to bring about a new status quo. That involves, but is not limited to, non-lethal engagements and coordination with former enemies. Under current U.S. Code, it is illegal for military operators to explore options that involve coordinating with or supporting listed terrorists. In essence, viable options to bring about timely resolution and stability are removed. This contributes to protracted efforts and renders assimilation of former terrorists more challenging. Time, public perception, and discourse are key factors in organizations known for employing terrorism to assimilate back into the international community. This is primarily achieved through military and political leaders meeting and coordinating efforts with former opponents. The following chapter focuses on case studies of MEK and Hamas, both currently listed on the FTOL, and the effects anti-terror definitions have on military options for engaging them.

Chapter III: Case Studies

This chapter consists of case studies of two organizations, both currently listed as terrorists by the U.S. Department of State, and both trying to gain legitimacy within the international community. The purpose is to assess the impact the U.S. Code definitions of terrorism has on military operations in COIN and stability environments.

Mujahedin-e Khalq

Enter the words Mujahedin-e Khalq (MEK) into a U.S. library database and the phrases that populate the screen are of the kind: "policy conundrum," "government paradox", and—of particular interest to this monograph—"protected terrorist." Further research reveals a group that has indirectly highlighted a U.S. national policy overlap. This overlap, also referred to as a bureaucratic snafu or gap, results in political situations where a nation categorizes a group as an ally and a foe simultaneously. This case study consists of an abbreviated MEK history, its interaction with coalition forces, and what effect, if any, the terrorist label has on military operations.

History of the Mujahedin-e Khalq

Mujahedin-e Khalq means the People's Holy Warriors and was founded in the 1960s by leftist students who wanted to change the regime in Iran. Their leftist ideology kept them in the company of the Soviet Union, Cuba, and East Germany for the majority of the 1960s and 70s. In the pursuit of their interests, these students conducted several attacks against Iranian government officials and eventually played a key role in the 1979 Islamic Revolution.[97]

In addition to their role in the 1979 revolution and links with communism, the MEK was involved in the assassinations of U.S. military personnel, civilian technicians working in Iran, and the hostage situation in the U.S. Embassy.[98] More to the point, they were opposed to the U.S backed Shah of Iran and played an instrumental role in the capitulation of his regime. The ending of the Islamic Revolution resulted in the ascendance of Ayatollah Khomeini, who immediately severed any agreement he had with the MEK and began efforts to weaken the group.

The severing of relations between the Ayatollah and the MEK resulted in a bloody conflict that forced many of the MEK's members to move to France and continue the struggle against the Ayatollah from there. Fluctuating degrees of support provided by the French government proved taxing on the MEK and in 1986 the group moved to Iraq, joined forces with Saddam Hussein, and continued its struggle against the Iranian regime. The alliance with Saddam branded the MEK as traitors with the Persians and cost them needed support from the Iranian population required to continue their struggle against the Iranian regime. The alliance with Saddam and the ways in which he employed them, coupled with activities in the 1970s and 80s, resulted in the group being listed on the FTOL in 1997.[99]

---

[97] Jeremiah E. Goulka, *The Mujahedin-e Khalq in Iraq: A Policy Conundrum* (Santa Monica, CA: Rand, 2009), 105.
[98] Ibid.82.
[99] The Iran Primer, "U.S. Terrorism Report: MEK and Jundallah," The United States Institute of Peace, http://iranprimer.usip.org/blog/2011/aug/23/us-terrorism-report-mek-and-jundallah (accessed September 13, 2011).

The MEK continued to fight a low-intensity conflict with the Iranian Regime until the 2003 United States invasion of Iraq. Coalition forces bombed MEK camps until they eventually agreed to a cease-fire on April 13, 2003.[100] Prior to the cease-fire, U.S. ground forces engaged MEK fighters and noticed a higher level of discipline and organization when compared to the Iraqi forces previously encountered in the war.[101] The MEK renounced violence at the signing of a second cease-fire in May 2003 and its members are currently working hard to remove their name from the State Department's FTOL.[102]

Interaction with Coalition Forces

United States Army Special Forces and official U.S. Army history both state that MEK engaged coalition forces during the 2003 invasion and posed a formidable threat with excellent fighting abilities.[103] The initial introduction between the U.S. ground forces and MEK fighters occurred while both were shooting at each other. Until the skirmish with MEK fighters, ground forces knew very little about them, outside of the fact that they were a fighting wing of Saddam's Army. As a result, U.S. Central Command (USCENTCOM) ordered the MEK to "capitulate" and "disarm"—a general order to surrender.

During surrender talks, MEK leadership spoke fluent English, to the surprise of the coalition negotiating team, and made claims of U.S. affiliation—most of which proved false. Placing their best foot forward, the MEK offered their services to coalition

---

[100] Goulka, *The Mujahedin-e Khalq in Iraq: A Policy Conundrum*, 105.
[101] Ibid., 10.
[102] Ibid.
[103] Ibid.

forces, which included but was not limited to, providing intelligence on Iran and aid in securing the border. The negotiators, impressed by their capabilities and willingness to support coalition efforts, agreed to a cease-fire instead of the surrender ordered by USCENTCOM.[104]

The cease-fire allowed the MEK to retain their weapons and confined them to designated bases. The MEK, later confronted by coalition negotiators to change from a cease-fire to surrender status, once again displayed their negotiating prowess and the coalition, on May 10, 2003, signed a new cease-fire agreement with the MEK.[105] In the new agreement, the MEK conceded to some minor adjustments—one of which required consolidation onto Camp Ashraf in Diyala Province, Iraq. The Secretary of Defense, Donald Rumsfeld, in June 2004, went beyond a cease fire agreement and designated the MEK as protected civilians under the Fourth Geneva Convention.[106] The Department of Defense designated the MEK protected civilians because Iraq had plans, after the official transfer of authority from coalition forces in 2004, to deport the MEK to Iran.

The Effect on Military Operations

To recap the MEK quagmire, an elite military group, under the Saddam regime, began working with the United States after the 2003 Iraq war, and was later designated "protected" by the Department of Defense,[107] all while listed as terrorists by the State

---

[104] Ibid., 11.
[105] Ibid.
[106] Ibid.
[107] Ibid.

Department.[108] In the midst of this policy paradox and legal quagmire are U.S. military operators protecting—albeit willingly—an organization listed as terrorists by their own government.

The coalition entered Iraq in 2003 with fewer forces than would be ideal for a regime change or a nation-building mission.[109] With limited forces and an expanding mission requirement, military operators—already impressed with MEK performance—saw the benefits of having an organization like this to aid in the stabilization process of Iraq. Their well-maintained vehicles where close to U.S. standards and could be used to augment coalition patrols, especially in the sparse boarder region with Iran. Not only did they speak fluent English, they spoke all the dialects common to the region between Iraq and Iran. For military operators accustomed to working in asymmetric environments, it seldom got better than this: to have a disciplined, proficient, organized force, indigenous to the area, volunteering their service.

In addition to the needed augmentation in troop strength, the MEK offered to use its network of informants deep within Iran to provide information to the U.S. Defense Department about Iran's nuclear facilities. With such lucrative offers, the MEK quickly gained support within the Department of Defense, but the fact that the Defense Department was making deals with a terrorist group did not go unnoticed by the Department of State.

The Department of State pointed out that military leaders have no authority to enter into arrangements that allow a designated terrorist group to not only keep their

---

[108] Ibid.
[109] Metz and Army War College . Strategic Studies Institute, *Rethinking Insurgency*, 69.

weapons, but also work in tandem with U.S. forces.[110] In essence, military forces coordinating with the MEK were breaking federal law. This placed military leaders in a precarious situation. The law is clear in regards to association with terrorists, but conditions on the ground warranted an unorthodox approach.

The special operations historical notes from Operation Iraqi Freedom observed that legal issues concerning the application of laws towards non-state terrorists were often redirected to the Defense Department.[111] This was the case with the MEK and as a result, the Defense Department issued one set of directives to the military, while the law dictated another. The legal dichotomy reached the zenith in 2004 when the Secretary of Defense designated the MEK protected persons.

In addition to the obvious contradiction of a nation protecting individuals it designated as terrorists and the legal argument that the Fourth Geneva Convention does not apply to the MEK because it engaged U.S. forces,[112] the U.S. military may have lost an opportunity to take full advantage of the MEK's potential. The MEK's network of supporters in Iran and its ability to provide intelligence diminish with each day it does not have the means to maintain its connection with Iran. The terrorist designation resulted in disarming of the MEK by coalition forces. In doing so, the MEK no longer had the ability to help secure the already porous border with Iran or aid in COIN operations within Iraq. This further increased the burden on coalition forces while removing a valuable intelligence asset.

---

[110] Goulka, *The Mujahedin-e Khalq in Iraq: A Policy Conundrum*, 105.
[111] Ibid., 19.
[112] The Iran Primer, *U.S. Terrorism Report: MEK and Jundallah*, 1.

As the coalition footprint in Iraq grew smaller, the newly elected Iraqi Government began to see an amicable relationship with Iran as being in their best interest. The MEK's repatriation to Iran may serve as a step towards that amicability. Leaving the MEK's fate to the Iraqis places the MEK at risk and potentially denies the United States of a capable asset against Iran at a time when the Iranian regime is working diligently on its nuclear program.

In summary, the checkered past of the MEK resulted in the organization being viewed as an ally and a foe by separate branches of the U.S. government. The terrorist categorization degraded the capability and support the MEK could provide military operators. The support had the potential to provide valuable resources to counter the Iraq insurgency that began in late 2003 and secure the border between Iraq and Iran. Fully explored, the MEK could reduce the time needed to defeat the insurgency—saving lives and money for the United States and Iraq.

Hamas

Hamas is an organization that has increased its legitimacy in the international community over the years, despite the protests of Israel and the United States. With growing international support and a number of recent victories, both political and military, Hamas has positioned itself to be a key player in the region. Once again the United States is faced with a policy conundrum. It has officially listed Hamas as a terrorist organization, but it's becoming more evident that it will have to begin talks with Hamas. The structure of this case study is similar to the MEK case study in order to facilitate direct comparison. It will consist of an abbreviated history, interaction with coalition forces, and what effect, if any, the terrorist label has on military operations.

History of Hamas

Hamas is an acronym for Harakat al-Muqawama al-Islamiya, or the Islamic Resistance Movement.[113] Resistance in this context means a never ending struggle requiring total effort by all. The organization derived from the Egypt-based Muslim Brotherhood. The Brotherhood was founded in Ismailiya, Egypt, in 1928, by an Egyptian schoolteacher named Hassan al-Banna. Hamas was established in 1968 as the Palestinian wing of the Brotherhood.[114] Hamas, as known today, converted its name in December 1987 with the main objective of eliminating the State of Israel. An additional aim for the group is to counter the secularization and westernization of Arab society.

Hamas developed its own name—though never denying its parent organization the Brotherhood—to become a national organization with international legitimacy and influence. In 2006, the head of Hamas political bureau, Khaled Mishal, stated that it is crucial that Hamas gain and maintain control by legal means.[115] Doing so will facilitate its aim of gaining and maintaining national status as well as international legitimacy.

Hamas uses three interrelated sections to help maintain their legal status and increase their influence in the region.[116] The first is social welfare and politics, the second is their paramilitary wing, and the third is an executive body that oversees all operations. Staying true to its purpose, Hamas' military wing began strikes against Israel the same year of its establishment and executed its first suicide car bomb on April 16, 1993 in the

---

[113] Matthew Levitt and Washington Institute for Near East Policy, *Hamas: Politics, Charity, and Terrorism in the Service of Jihad* (New Haven: Yale University Press, 2006), 324.
[114] Ibid.
[115] Ibid.
[116] Ibid.

44

West Bank.[117] That was followed by another suicide car bomb in Israel on April 6, 1994. Since its inception, Hamas continued to focus its attacks on Israelis, committing a range of attacks from mortar strikes on Israeli occupied territories to kidnapping and murders of Jewish soldiers and civilians. From September 2000 through March 2004, Hamas conducted over 425 attacks against Israel causing more than 2,450 casualties.[118]

Hamas champions its attacks against Israel as a sign of its commitment to the Palestinian people and a viable alternative to the Palestinian Authority (P.A.).[119] Hamas seized on the lack of trust and rampant corruption in the P.A. and began targeted social programs that improved the basic living standards of the demographic most frustrated with the P.A.[120] Evidence to support the population's frustration with the P.A surfaced in the Municipal elections in May 2005, which resulted in Hamas winning five of seven council seats.[121] Research conducted by Levitt, a senior fellow from the Washington Institute for Near East Policy, suggested that Hamas did not win on its violence towards Israel alone. Its social services, known also as social dawa, played a significant role as well. Hamas provided basic staples such as rice and sugar to the poor and is perceived by the public to lack the rampant corruption of the Palestinian Authority.[122] Realizing the success of their social dawa, Hamas expanded services to the people of Palestine, often providing essential services that should be provided by the state, such as health care,

---

[117] Ibid.

[118] Ibid., 12.

[119] Paul Wilkinson, *Terrorism Versus Democracy: The Liberal State Response*, Vol. 9 (London ; Portland, OR: Frank Cass, 2000), 255.

[120] Levitt and Washington Institute for Near East Policy, *Hamas: Politics, Charity, and Terrorism in the Service of Jihad*, 17.

[121] Ibid.

[122] Wilkinson, *Terrorism Versus Democracy: The Liberal State Response*, 255.

education supplies, and infrastructure support.[123] With an unemployment rate of 33.5 percent, a large portion of the population responded well to the Hamas dawa programs and in January 2006, Hamas won 44.5 percent of the vote and became the majority party in Palestine, achieving its national status. [124]

Interaction with Coalition Forces

The U.S. military's interaction with Hamas and its military arm has been mainly through indirect methods. That indirect interaction is largely via its parent organization the Muslim Brotherhood.[125] This is due in large part because there are currently no conventional U.S forces in Palestine. The Muslim brotherhood on the other hand has clear connections to coalition forces that have operated or continue to operate in places like Egypt and Libya because of the Arab Spring.[126]

The Arab Spring, also known as the Arab Awakening, began in the winter of 2010 when Mohamed Bouazizi committed self-immolation in Tunisia to protest his harsh treatment by the police.[127] It has resulted in the United States making alliances that contradicts its own policy. United States forces, serving as a member of a coalition of forces, coordinated with and supported protesting civilians, that later became splintered

---

[123] Ibid.

[124] Levitt and Washington Institute for Near East Policy, *Hamas: Politics, Charity, and Terrorism in the Service of Jihad*, 245.

[125] Marr et al., *Human Terrain Mapping: A Critical Step to Winning the COIN Fight*, 4.

[126] Ibid.

[127] Garry Blight and Sheila Pulham, "Arab Spring: An Interactive Timeline of Middle East Protests," The Guardian, http://www.guardian.co.uk/world/interactive/2011/mar/22/middle-east-protest-interactive-timeline (accessed July, 2011).

rebel forces (insurgents) with ties to terrorism.[128] The Muslim Brotherhood represents the executive arm and council for these rebel forces. It also serves as council to the Egyptian military for foreign and regional diplomacy.[129] The Brotherhood is currently preparing for parliamentary and presidential elections to consolidate its recent success gained by the insurgency in Egypt and Libya.[130] This success has also led to the opening of the barrier gate that separated Gaza from Egypt and the receiving of Hamas leaders as government officials.[131] This demonstrates to the international community the bond between Hamas and the Brotherhood, while further legitimizing both. Increasing legitimacy in the global community for Hamas and the Brotherhood means state level cooperation with the United States is becoming more likely.

The decision to support the Arab Spring and with it the Muslim Brotherhood is a violation of U.S. law. The Brotherhood's umbilical relationship to Hamas renders all degrees of coordination and support—especially money—to the Brotherhood illegal, according to the U.S. Code. The monetary support to the Arab Spring provided by the United States and Europe is roughly $40 Billion,[132] some of which will ineluctably benefit the Brotherhood and Hamas by default. In addition, the U.S. Department of State has a policy of not dealing—in any way—with terror organizations or their affiliates in order to deny them the recognition and legitimacy they often seek. The State

---

[128] Walid Phares, "Muslim Brotherhood Riding the Crest of Arab Spring," Newsmax, http://www.newsmax.com/walidphares/muslimbrotherhood-arabspring-gadhafi/2011/06/03/id/398700 (accessed July 14, 2011).

[129] Marr et al., *Human Terrain Mapping: A Critical Step to Winning the COIN Fight*, 4.

[130] Phares, *Muslim Brotherhood Riding the Crest of Arab Spring*, 1.

[131] Levitt and Washington Institute for Near East Policy, *Hamas: Politics, Charity, and Terrorism in the Service of Jihad*, 324.

[132] Phares, *Muslim Brotherhood Riding the Crest of Arab Spring*, 1.

Department's recent dealings with the Brotherhood is therefore a contradiction of its own policy.

Some allies of the United States appear to not value or agree with the terrorist categorization. Nations such as Saudi Arabia and Qatar provide a preponderance (over 40 percent) of the funding received by Hamas.[133] Despite this contradicting view of Hamas, both Saudi Arabia and Qatar have U.S. military bases within their borders that support operations in the Middle East.

The Effect on Military Operations

The military operations that deal with, or have dealt with, Hamas are rare and seldom included conventional ground forces. As a result, the legal quagmire often associated with operations involving terrorist groups—such as the MEK—was less of an issue with Hamas. The recent increase in contact between the brotherhood and U.S forces is due primarily to the Arab Spring. The Arab Spring[134] resulted in support to organizations tied to Hamas, and an indirect relationship between the U.S. military and Hamas.

Barring special operations forces, the military's role in support to the Arab Spring has been primarily through air support.[135] Air support requires coordination and de-confliction to provide accurate servicing of targets in order to nest effects from air with

---

[133] Levitt and Washington Institute for Near East Policy, *Hamas: Politics, Charity, and Terrorism in the Service of Jihad*, 324.

[134] Robert Naiman, "USA, Muslim Brotherhood Take Steps Towards Accomodations," Huffington Post, http://www.huffingtonpost.com/robert-naiman/reset-usa-muslim-brotherh_b_818925.html (accessed September 03, 2011).

[135] Ibid.

operations on the ground. Members of the U.S. military, as a result, planned and executed targets in conjunction with rebel leaders in nations such as Libya.[136]

Hamas and its umbrella organization the Muslim Brotherhood were a known part of the rebel organization but received support from the United States none-the-less during combat operations in Libya.[137] The mission was to provide limited air and ground support to rebel forces.[138] The supporting role absolved military members of the support to terrorism restrictions because the approval was at the State Department level and not within the Department of Defense.

The tension, traditionally carried by the military leaders, rested at the state level for Arab Spring uprising involving Hamas and the Muslim Brotherhood. The tension derives from having to decide whether to seize on a strategic opportunity, such as the Middle East democratic movement, or remain within the confines of domestic legal definitions.[139] Military operators directed to provide support, were free to explore a wide array of viable options that would be restricted under traditional circumstances.

In closing, the Hamas conundrum serves as a firsthand example for state level leaders of the tension that exists for military operators facing the challenge of how to work within the constraints of laws that have jurisdiction in—but are not germane to—combat environments. The DoS violated its own established policies on terrorism to support a national strategic objective and in doing so raised a question as to the relevancy of those policies in the first place. In essence, the need for a state to exercise legal

---

[136] Marr et al., *Human Terrain Mapping: A Critical Step to Winning the COIN Fight*, 4.
[137] Naiman, *USA, Muslim Brotherhood Take Steps Towards Accomodations*, 1.
[138] Ibid.
[139] Phares, *Muslim Brotherhood Riding the Crest of Arab Spring*, 1.

exemption of its own established laws on terrorism for combat operations demonstrates the incongruity of such laws and its definitions in combat.

Conclusion

The intent of this monograph is not to defend terrorist behavior or the logic behind such actions. The intent is to assess the relevancy of having terror laws applied in a combat environment. As stated in chapter one, the purpose of the laws surrounding terrorism is to aid in the protection of U.S. citizens and its national interest. It also aids in the nesting of operations between the United States and its allies against terror organizations. Taken in the proper context, the laws allow for the prosecution of individuals who declare themselves as enemies of the United States. The intended focus of this research is how the blanket application of the law, applied out of context, can adversely affect operations in combat.

There is no indication that the U.S. Congress, when enacting the laws that govern terrorism, foresaw conventional forces fighting an asymmetric war, with a direct connection to domestic policies. The analysis of what is defined by U.S. Code as terrorism, the legal ramifications associated with the definition, and study of the effect on military operations led to an evaluation of issues surrounding the laws. The crux of the issue surrounding the law and its influence on military operations rests in the definition of the term "terrorist" and "acts of terror." Scholars and nations struggle to objectively define who a terrorist is and what constitutes acts of terror. Most nations and scholars, as demonstrated by the United Nations' panel, simply accept the fact that a unanimous definition of a terrorist cannot be reached. The term is too subjective and politically charged to ever achieve unanimity. The subjective nature of the definition also renders the application of U.S. Code in combat difficult. In a combat environment, people and organizations do not adhere to civil codes intended for stable lawful societies because the violent nature of war precludes such lawful behavior. Environments where counter-insurgency and stability operations are conducted are, generally speaking, poor, war torn, and lawless.

In environments where national authority cannot enforce the rule of law, individual citizens engage in acts they determine will secure themselves and their families. Through a western lens, these acts appear deplorable, inexcusable, and undeserving of consideration for objective analysis. The military operator must, however, attempt to view acts by individuals holistically and contextually in order to conduct meaningful analysis. In other words, in a combat environment, the influential nature and public view of key actors may be more valuable to the mission than deplorable acts they committed in pursuit of their interests.

The Sunni Awakening serves as a modern day example of how conditions can change drastically in COIN conflicts, resulting in new alliances or coordination with groups that once opposed each other. The military operator requires the flexibility to make such coordination or alliance in order to exploit a change in conditions. Timely action during a change in condition can prove conducive to mission accomplishment. If military operators had followed the letter of the law concerning terrorism, no coordination or alliances would have been made with Iraqi Sunnis, who at that time met almost every U.S. Code criteria for a terror organization. The coordination resulted in efficient defeat of a violent insurgency and the expulsion of Al-Qaeda from Iraq. Should opportunities like the Sunni Awakening occur in future operations military leaders require operational leeway to exercise viable options that facilitate mission success.

As described in chapter two, and again illustrated by the Sunni Awakening, terrorism is a strategy and when no longer strategically beneficial, it may be abandoned for more effective measures. Once a group makes the decision to no longer use terrorism and attempts to assimilate into the global community, cooperation from military and political leaders is required. Time, discourse, and public perception facilitate the assimilation of terror organizations into the global community. Reluctance by a nation to cooperate with former perpetrators of terrorism, due to strict adherence to civilian legal codes, may serve to work against the desired end-state of that nation. The Arab spring would not have been possible or it would not have occurred so efficiently without the cooperation of Sunnis and coalition forces in Iraq.

Throughout history, terrorism has been used by different cultures to serve varying interests. Terrorism is not organic to one nation, culture, or region. Representatives from all cultures have used it at one point or another in order to produce a desired result. Through this understanding, acts of terror can be separated from the logic that employs it. Separation will allow for independent but concurrent lethal and nonlethal targeting of the act itself and the cognitive thought process that adapts it. Take for example a farmer who plants a bomb at a government building because his crops—and with it a means to provide for his family—were accidentally destroyed by coalition forces. Lethal means may be used to neutralize the threat of the farmer with the bomb, while nonlethal civil projects to rebuild his farm and his neighbor's farm begin. The lethal action demonstrates that there are repercussions for extreme acts of violence at the same time the non-lethal action reduces the chance of another farmer adapting a similar tactic. Other farmers contemplating drastic actions may choose to reconcile their grievances in a diplomatic manner.

As illustrated by the MEK and Hamas case studies, most organizations that commit acts of terror are not aimless entities determined to cause anarchy. In the case of MEK, they represent an organization categorized by events over three decades ago during a turbulent time in Iran. Since then, their interests have grown more in line with that of the United States. Hamas, on the other hand, is determined to see the fall of Israel and has gained legitimacy through provincial elections and the recent Arab Spring which increased the popularity of its parent organization the Muslim Brotherhood.

The MEK has demonstrated its value and willingness to work with the United States against Iran but the terrorist categorization, has prevented the full use of MEK capabilities. The United States chose to work with the Muslim Brotherhood in order to support the democratic movement in the Middle East, but their umbilical relationship to the terror organization Hamas has resulted in a contradiction of policy. The MEK and Hamas case studies represent real world examples of why terrorist categorizations are not germane in combat because they lack context. Through context, definitions develop meaning and understanding. Understanding then leads to better targeting of key actors and employment of resources to achieve the desired end-state.

Based on the information gathered during this research, it is recommended that the U.S. Code regarding anti terrorism be amended to limit the jurisdiction to non-combat environments. This will allow the military, with its broader contextual understanding, to assess key actors with the circumstances of their behavior and engage them accordingly. This degree of operational latitude will result in timely action when conditions become favorable and aid in judicious achievement of the desired end-state.

Bibliography

Congress. *Definition of Terrorism.* 101. no. Title 22, (1989, 1988): 2656f(d),265f(d).

104th Congress. "Title 18, Crimes and Criminal Procedures, Sec. 2339A. Providing Material Support to Terrorists." Office of the Law Revision Counsel, U.S. House of Representatives. http://uscode.house.gov/uscode-cgi/fastweb.exe?getdoc+uscview+t17t20+1114+36++%28%29%20%20AND%20%28USC%20w%2F10%20%2818%20U.S.C.%20§%202339A%29%29%3ACITE%20%20%20%20%20%20%20%20 (accessed July, 2011).

Allison, Graham T. and Philip Zelikow. *Essence of Decision: Explaining the Cuban Missile Crisis.* SAMS Reserve -- First Floor. 2nd ed. New York: Longman, 1999.

Benjamin, Daniel and Steven Simon. *The Age of Sacred Terror.* 1st ed. New York: Random, 2002.

Blight, Garry and Pulham, Sheila. "Arab Spring: An Interactive Timeline of Middle East Protests." The Guardian. http://www.guardian.co.uk/world/interactive/2011/mar/22/middle-east-protest-interactive-timeline (accessed July, 2011).

Carr, Matthew. *The Infernal Machine: A History of Terrorism.* New York: New Press, 2006.

Cordesman, Anthony H. and Center for Strategic and International Studies. *Terrorism, Asymmetric Warfare, and Weapons of Mass Destruction: Defending the U.S. Homeland.* Westport, Conn.: Praeger, 2002.

Cox, Dan G., John Falconer, and Brian Stackhouse. *Terrorism, Instability, and Democracy in Asia and Africa.* CGSC Faculty Publication. Hanover, NH: University Press of New England, 2009.

Department of Defense. *Joint Publication 3-26, Counterterrorism.* Washington, DC: Department of Defense, 2009.

Files, Terrorism. "The History of Terrorism." Nabou. www.terrorismfiles.org/encyclopedia/history2011).

Gill, Terry D. and Dieter Fleck. *Handbook of the International Law of Military Operations.* Oxford ; New York: Oxford University Press, 2010.

Gottlieb, Stuart. *Debating Terrorism and Counterterrorism: Conflicting Perspectives on Causes, Contexts, and Responses.* Washington, DC: CQ Press, 2010.

Goulka, Jeremiah E. *The Mujahedin-e Khalq in Iraq: A Policy Conundrum*. Santa Monica, CA: Rand, 2009.

Hall, Mimi. "U.S. has Mandela on Terrorist List." USA Today. http://www.usatoday.com/news/world/2008-04-30-watchlist_N.htm (accessed July, 2011).

Hill, Charles W. L. *International Business, Competing in the Global Marketplace*. Edited by Brent Gordon. 8th ed. Vol. One. Washington: McGraw-Hill, 2011.

Hoffman, Bruce. *Inside Terrorism*. Sams : Scoa. Rev a expa ed. New York: Columbia University Press, 2006.

Howard, Russell D., Reid L. Sawyer, and Barry R. McCaffrey. *Terrorism and Counterterrorism: Understanding the New Security Environment : Readings & Interpretations*. Guilford, CT: McGraw-Hill, 2002.

Juergensmeyer, Mark and Inc NetLibrary. *Terror in the Mind of God*. Comparative Studies in Religion and Society. Vol. 13. Berkeley: University of California Press, 2000.

Kuhn, Thomas S. *The Structure of Scientific Revolutions*. SAMS : Design. 3rd ed. Chicago, Ill.: University of Chicago Press, 1996.

Kushner, Harvey W. "Japanese Red Army." Encyclopedia of Terrorism. www.google.books/books (accessed November 24, 2011).

Levitt, Matthew and Washington Institute for Near East Policy. *Hamas: Politics, Charity, and Terrorism in the Service of Jihad*. Sams : Tcc. New Haven: Yale University Press, 2006.

Lynn, John A. *Battle: A History of Combat and Culture*. Sams : Toa. Rev a updat ed. Cambridge, MA: Westview Press, 2004.

Marr, Jack, John Cushing, Brandon Garner, and Richard Thompson. "Human Terrain Mapping: A Critical Step to Winning the COIN Fight." *Military Review* 1 (June 28, 2011, 2008): 4.

Martin, Gus. *Understanding Terrorism: Challenges, Perspectives, and Issues*. A529 Course Reserve. 3rd ed. Los Angeles: Sage, 2010.

Metz, Steven and Army War College . Strategic Studies Institute. *Rethinking Insurgency*. Washington, D.C.: Congressional Research Service, Library of Congress, 2007.

Naiman, Robert. "USA, Muslim Brotherhood Take Steps Towards Accomodations."
Huffington Post. http://www.huffingtonpost.com/robert-naiman/reset-usa-muslim-
brotherh_b_818925.html (accessed September 03, 2011).

Office of the Coordinator for Counterterrorism. "U.S. State Department Foreign Terrorist
Organization List." U.S. Department of State.
http://www.state.gov/s/ct/rls/other/des/123085.htm (accessed September, 2011).

O'Neill, Bard E. *Insurgency and Terrorism: From Revolution to Apocalypse*. 2nd ed.
Washington, D.C.: Potomac Books, 2005.

Osborn, William M. *The Wild Frontier*. 1st ed. Vol. 1. New York: Random House, 2000.

Pape, Robert Anthony. *Dying to Win: The Strategic Logic of Suicide Terrorism*. 1st ed.
New York: Random House, 2005.

Pearlman, Michael D. "The American Revolutionary War: A Complex "Little Conflict"
on the Edge of "the Civilized World"." *US Army Command and General Staff
College* 3, no. 3 (November 2010, 2010): 61-82.

Phares, Walid. "Muslim Brotherhood Riding the Crest of Arab Spring." Newsmax.
http://www.newsmax.com/walidphares/muslimbrotherhood-arabspring-
gadhafi/2011/06/03/id/398700 (accessed July 14, 2011).

Pillar, Paul R. and Inc ebrary. *Terrorism and U.S. Foreign Policy*. Washington, D.C.:
Brookings Institution Press, 2001.

Porter, Patrick. *Military Orientalism: Eastern War through Western Eyes*. Sams : Toa.
New York: Columbia University Press, 2009.

Record, Jeffrey. *Beating Goliath: Why Insurgencies Win*. Sams : Eoa. Washington, D.C.:
Potomac Books, 2009.

Ruby, Charles L. "The Definition of Terrorism." *Analysis of Social Issues and Public
Policy* (2002): 9,9-14.

Talbott, Strobe and Nayan Chanda. *The Age of Terror: America and the World After
September 11*. A529 Course Reserve. 1st ed. New York: Basic Books : Yale Center
for the Study of Globalization, 2001.

The Iran Primer. "U.S. Terrorism Report: MEK and Jundallah." The United States
Institute of Peace. http://iranprimer.usip.org/blog/2011/aug/23/us-terrorism-report-
mek-and-jundallah (accessed September 13, 2011).

Thompson, Loren B. *Low-Intensity Conflict: The Pattern of Warfare in the Modern World*. Georgetown International Security Studies Series. Lexington, Mass.: Lexington Books, 1989.

United Nation. "Press Conference by Head of Counter-Terrorism Committee Executive Directorate." Department of Public Information, News and Media Division, New York. http://www.un.org/News/briefings/docs/2010/101201_CTED.doc.htm (accessed August 20, 2011).

———. "AD HOC Committee Negotiating Comprehensive Anti-Terrorism." Department of Public Information, News and Media Division, New York. http://www.un.org/News/Press/docs/2007/L3112.doc.htm (accessed August 20, 2011).

Wilkinson, Paul. *Terrorism Versus Democracy: The Liberal State Response*. A529 Course Reserve. Vol. 9. London ; Portland, OR: Frank Cass, 2000.